Why do we need maths?

Written by Peter Gallivan

Contents

Collins

1 What is maths?

Maths is everywhere, so it's important to know about! From making trains run on time to landing a robot on Mars, you'll find maths is a part of most of our modern world if you look hard enough. This is why it's one of the first things people learn about at school.

Think about a trip to the supermarket. Do you have enough money to get a chocolate bar with the rest of your shopping? How many apples will make up one kilogram? You need maths to be able to answer these questions.

The supermarket is one of the many places we use maths every day.

But what actually is maths? Put simply, it's a set of tools which can be used to explore how the world works. These tools are not just used by **mathematicians**, but by scientists, **engineers, accountants** – just about everyone really!

The maths people use today has been slowly developed over thousands of years, by mathematicians working all across the world.

The ancient Greeks made many maths discoveries we still use today.

A short history of maths

20,000 BCE: Central Africa

An animal bone was found in 1950, believed to be from 20,000 BCE, in the ruins of an ancient village. It had human-made markings on it and is the oldest evidence of maths. It is thought to be a simple calendar.

3000 BCE: Mesopotamia

This ancient **civilisation** was the first to develop a written way of counting. They used this to study how the planets moved in the sky.

UK

Europe

ancient Greece

ancient Egypt

Central Africa

2500 BCE: ancient Egypt

The Egyptians carefully measured their land and buildings. Their understanding of area and volume helped them to build giant **structures** like the pyramids.

500 BCE: ancient Greece

Greek **philosophers** developed **theories** to explain how the world worked. They showed that numbers could be used to understand mysteries, like why the stars appeared to move in the sky.

800 CE: Iraq and the Arab world

Mathematicians in the Arab world came up with many ideas we still use today, including the numerals one to nine. These made it much easier to do complicated maths.

1700 CE: Europe

This time was called the Enlightenment in Europe. This was the birth of science as we know it today: using maths to study the details of the world, and to improve the lives of people.

Mesopotamia

Iraq

1815 CE: UK

Ada Lovelace, a British mathematician and daughter of famous poet Lord Byron, used mathematical ideas to write the first computer program – a series of codes a machine can follow to do a specific job.

1912 CE: UK

Alan Turing, a British mathematician and code breaker, suggested that a computer might be able to learn and program itself. This is what we now call artificial intelligence.

How do we use maths?

To do anything with maths, you need data. Data simply means information that someone has collected – it could be the number of cars on a street, the number of people in a class or how much it rained in a day. Maths is the study of numbers, and collecting data is how mathematicians turn the world into numbers.

Once you have collected some data, you're ready to do some maths. Here are some common ways maths can be used to understand the world. You probably know how to do some of these already!

Displaying data

Displaying data in a graph or chart – this is much easier than looking at a long list of numbers.

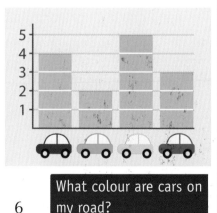

What colour are cars on my road?

Averages

Working out the average or the middle number in a range of numbers – this helps people to quickly understand some data.

The average student in my class is 150 centimetres tall.

Finding patterns

Finding patterns in data that has been collected – this can be used to find problems or make plans.

Students aged 13 are taller than those aged eight.

Comparing data

Comparing data from different places, to understand why it differs.

It rains more in Sweden than in Egypt.

Predicting

Predicting the future using data from the past.

YESTERDAY TODAY TOMORROW

It will rain more tomorrow than it did today.

7

Maths mistake: a tale of two towers

Wood is used to make buildings all across the world because it's strong, lightweight and easily grown. But it's important to know that trees have water inside. Once they are chopped down, the wood slowly dries out and shrinks slightly.

In Chesterfield in the UK, there's a church with a strange-looking tower. It was built in 1360 with new, wet wood. As the wood dried in the sun it shrank, twisting the tower. The tower now leans almost three metres off to the side!

Today, the amount of water in wood is carefully measured before it is used for building, to make sure it's fully dried and won't cause any issues later. Wood is now used more than ever to make buildings, and some are almost 100 metres tall!

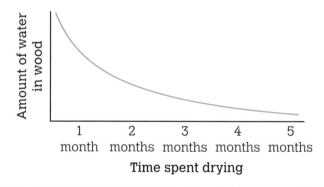

You wouldn't think that mistakes would still be made today when building towers, would you? But 20 Fenchurch Street, known as the Walkie Talkie Tower, was built in London, UK, in 2015 with an unexpected fault – when the sun shone, its curved glass surface acted like a magnifying glass and melted cars parked nearby! This very expensive mistake was fixed by fitting sunshades to the tower's surface.

2 Our unpredictable planet

Our planet can be very unpredictable, and the weather
most of all. In some places in the world, the weather can
change from being sunny with no clouds to heavy rainfall
in just a few minutes.

All weather on Earth is caused by heat from the Sun.
Warm air rises up and cold air moves in to fill the gaps.
This is what we feel as wind. The Sun **evaporates** water
from the surface of Earth. When this water vapour
in the air cools, it condenses to form clouds.
Eventually, the water droplets in the clouds become
too heavy and they fall to Earth as rain.

The weather in some places is very changeable.

Ushuaia, Argentina:
January 9.7 °C;
July 2.4 °C

In a particular place, weather is usually different from day to day, but year to year, it's generally the same. For example, in the UK, it's generally cold in the winter but warm in the summer. Scientists who study weather, called meteorologists, take measurements for many years and work out an average of what the weather will be like throughout the year. This is called the climate. Working out a place's climate is a useful way to know what sort of weather to expect at different times of the year.

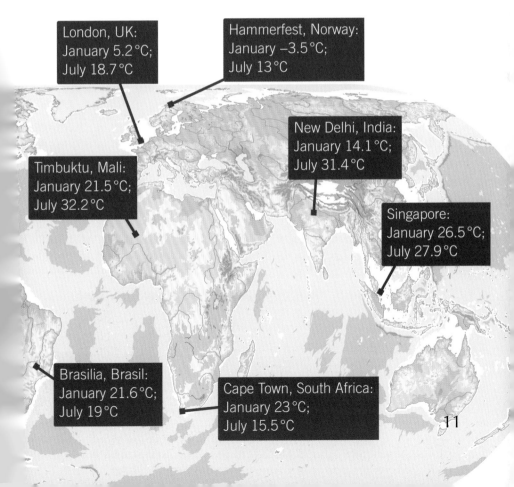

London, UK:
January 5.2 °C;
July 18.7 °C

Hammerfest, Norway:
January −3.5 °C;
July 13 °C

New Delhi, India:
January 14.1 °C;
July 31.4 °C

Timbuktu, Mali:
January 21.5 °C;
July 32.2 °C

Singapore:
January 26.5 °C;
July 27.9 °C

Brasilia, Brasil:
January 21.6 °C;
July 19 °C

Cape Town, South Africa:
January 23 °C;
July 15.5 °C

Rainfall ahead

Knowing a place's climate can be useful, but predicting exactly what the weather will be like at a set time is much more important. So much of what happens in the world relies on these predictions – so that traffic moves safely, farmers can successfully grow food and people are kept safe from floods and **hurricanes**.

Governments and companies spend huge amounts of money predicting the weather. Some of the biggest and most powerful computers in the world are used to do the complicated maths for this. This might seem like a lot of work just to tell you if you need an umbrella, but predicting the weather also keeps everyone around the world safe from our unpredictable planet.

Collecting lots of data is vital for weather forecasts to be accurate. All around the world, weather stations, weather balloons, aeroplanes and ships record the weather. There are also **satellites** in space which can measure how thick clouds are, to work out how much rain they have in them! All of this data is processed by computers which create a weather forecast.

Forecasting the weather for the next day is easy – if there's a large rain cloud approaching, it's straightforward to work out where it might move next, based on the speed of the wind. But predicting the weather for the next month is much more difficult, and the world's top mathematicians are always working hard to improve these forecasts.

This weather balloon carries a box filled with instruments to measure the weather, and can send information back to scientists via the internet.

In the eye of the storm

Sometimes collecting weather data needs a lot of bravery. Some of the bravest people are storm-chasers – specially trained people who drive very close to **tornadoes** and hurricanes, to get accurate measurements of what is happening in these extreme storms. Some people even fly aeroplanes through the centre of hurricanes! The data collected by storm-chasers helps scientists to understand better how storms grow and move, which means they can improve storm forecasts.

A storm-chaser drives towards a tornado.

Hurricanes are one of the most powerful types of weather on the planet, and special satellites monitor the skies, looking out for them. Once a hurricane is spotted, satellites send new data every 30 seconds to help track its movements.

This data is used to make maps showing where the hurricane might travel in the next five days, to help people know if they can safely stay in their house or not. But only the next 24 hours can be accurately predicted. The longer five-day forecast maps are called "cones of uncertainty", because of the way the predicted area gets wider further into the future.

a hurricane forecast map

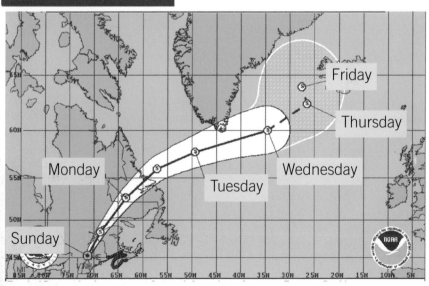

Over the past 100 years, measurements show that Earth's climate has been getting warmer year after year. This is called called **global warming**. This warming is happening fastest at the North and South Poles, causing the ice there to melt.

Wildfires burn in California, USA. 2020 was the worst year ever recorded for wildfires in the USA.

These higher temperatures are also making weather predictions harder. Hotter climates make extreme weather events like hurricanes, floods, droughts and wildfires happen more often and more severely. These events are more difficult to predict than everyday weather, making weather forecasting even more difficult.

Volcanic maths

In 79 CE, Mount Vesuvius in Italy erupted, burying the town of Pompeii and damaging other towns nearby. Although it was almost 2000 years ago, we know all about this eruption because it was written down in unusual detail by an 18-year-old called Pliny the Younger.

Before the volcano erupted, Pliny wrote that "There had been noticed for many days a trembling of the earth", and on the day of the eruption "a cloud of unusual size and appearance" appeared in the sky.

Pliny the Younger

At the time, these observations weren't connected to the volcano erupting, but today scientists understand that they are early signs, and can use these seemingly random events to predict when a volcano will erupt.

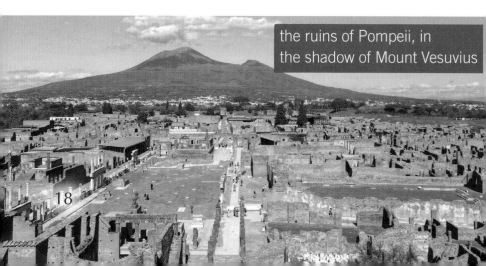

the ruins of Pompeii, in the shadow of Mount Vesuvius

Scientists constantly measure hundreds of volcanoes all around the world, even if they aren't erupting. By looking at all of this data together, they can find common things that happen before a volcano erupts, and use this information to predict when other volcanoes might erupt. We now have a good idea of the warning signs of a volcano erupting.

Warning signs that a volcano may erupt

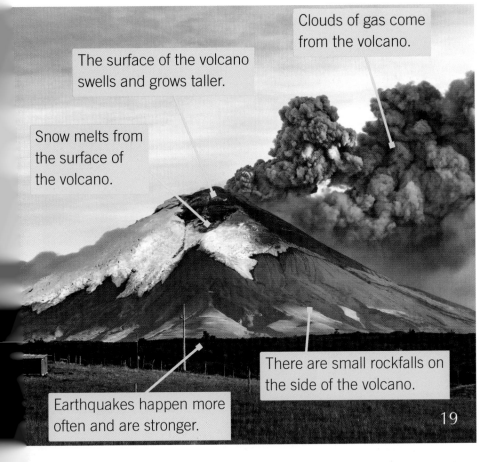

Clouds of gas come from the volcano.

The surface of the volcano swells and grows taller.

Snow melts from the surface of the volcano.

There are small rockfalls on the side of the volcano.

Earthquakes happen more often and are stronger.

Maths mistake: sinking ships

Sometimes it doesn't take extreme weather to make a maths mistake obvious – just a light breeze is enough! On 10th August 1628, the Swedish military launched a ship called the *Vasa*. It was designed to be the most powerful and impressive ship in the world, scaring off all others. It had **64** heavy **bronze** cannons, and stored **1000** cannonballs. The *Vasa* was covered in wooden carvings, painted in bright colours and gold leaf. It was built to have a full crew of **450** people.

This gigantic **69**-metre-long ship was built in only two years – very fast for the time. When it was finished, it weighed a colossal **1210** tonnes – that's the weight of over **170** adult elephants!

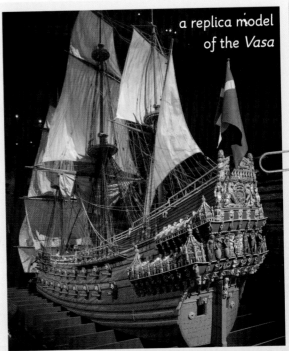

a replica model of the *Vasa*

When it finally launched, the waterfront in Stockholm was packed with people, excited to see this huge ship leave harbour. Sadly, a light gust of wind blew the ship over, and it almost immediately sank! It's easy to realise what went wrong if you look at the maths. The ship was too heavy, especially with all the cannons at the top, and its base was too narrow. This made it very unsteady, and very easy to blow over.

A similar mistake almost happened in 2013, when a new submarine was built in Spain that was too heavy to ever float! Thankfully, this was spotted before it was launched, otherwise it too would have sunk, just like the *Vasa*.

3 Maths in the city

Maths is used to carefully plan our towns and cities, to help make people's lives easier. How long do people have to walk to reach the nearest bus stop or train station? How often do they visit parks? How many bedrooms do people need in their houses? By collecting data and information on how people live and use cities, we can use maths to help make them better places to live in.

Sometimes these will be big decisions like where new buildings can go, or where to build new roads. Other decisions are small but can still have a huge impact on how a city runs, like the number of dustbins. Lots of problems can happen in a city if there aren't enough bins for people to use!

Modern cities like Tokyo are carefully planned.

22

In the past, cities were built without much planning, with new houses just built where there happened to be spare land. The Great Fire of London in 1666 showed how dangerous a badly planned city can be. This fire quickly spread through London because it was packed full of poorly built wooden houses.

Today, this wouldn't happen, as cities are planned to stop fires from spreading so easily between buildings.

The Great Fire of London destroyed over 13,000 houses.

23

Transport without delay

Being in charge of public transport for a city is
a difficult job! How would you decide where buses should
stop, or how many trains to run every hour? This is where
collecting data is vital. Most cities measure the number of
people at stations at different times of the day. This will
show when places are busiest, and so more trains can be
scheduled to run at this time. Trains can also drive past
stops which have no people at them, making everyone's
journey quicker.

Paris Gare du Nord is the busiest train station in Europe,
with over 200 million passengers every year.

Data can be used to make transport quicker for everyone, but that doesn't mean people will follow instructions. Holborn tube station in London discovered that making people stand still on escalators was quicker for everyone. This is because you can fit more people on an escalator standing still than walking, reducing time spent queuing to get on. But passengers didn't listen to the recommendation to stand still, as they felt walking on the escalator was faster, even though the maths showed they were wrong!

Holborn tube station has over 56 million passengers every year – that's a lot of escalator rides!

Most cities change their transport plans gradually, to avoid too much disruption. But in 2021, the city of Edmonton in Canada completely changed all of its bus routes and stops so that 93 per cent of people would live just five minutes' walk from a bus stop. Big changes like this can be confusing, but our cities are always growing and changing, so transport needs to adapt to keep up with this growth.

Virtual cities

Making changes to transport affects almost everyone in a city, so it's very important that any changes are planned properly. In Paris, the city government built a digital model of the city to test ideas. To do this, they collected a huge amount of data – where the roads, road signs and traffic lights were located, and how trains, buses, cars and even people moved about the city. This virtual city let them try out different ideas of improving transport to see what happens, before making changes in real life.

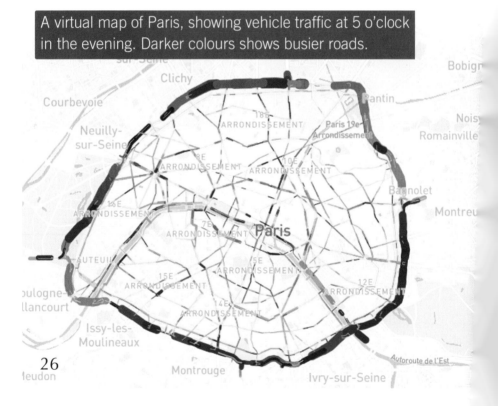

A virtual map of Paris, showing vehicle traffic at 5 o'clock in the evening. Darker colours shows busier roads.

By using a virtual model, city planners can make sure any changes work for everyone, from a child going to school on their bike, to a lorry driver delivering packages. For example, they can test to see if closing roads to make an area safer for **pedestrians** can happen without causing huge traffic jams on other streets. The biggest change in Paris was making a long stretch along the banks of the river Seine car-free. In the summer, this road is now a public beach, with cafés and bars where cars used to drive, and even real sand! More areas will soon be made car-free, helping to make Paris a safer and healthier city for everyone.

On this road in Paris, deckchairs now take the place of cars.

How to grow a city

All across the world, cities are growing, as more and more people move from the countryside to **urban** areas. To plan for the future, town planners look at data from the past to understand how fast each city is growing. They can then work out how the population will grow in the future, and build enough homes for everyone.

In many cities like Singapore, high-rise flats are used to provide homes for rapidly growing populations.

Singapore is a **city-state** based on a small island in Asia. Being an island, it doesn't have much space to grow, so the city has been carefully planned to make the best use of space, and fit the growing population.

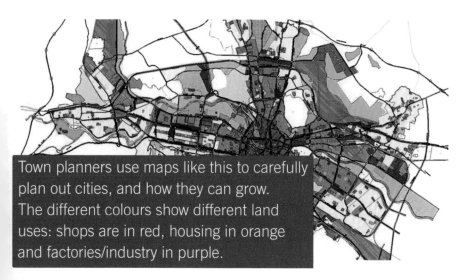

Town planners use maps like this to carefully plan out cities, and how they can grow. The different colours show different land uses: shops are in red, housing in orange and factories/industry in purple.

New houses are built on the edge of the city, centred around train stations. This encourages people to use public transport, and not rely on cars.

Most new homes are built as blocks of flats with up to 15 floors. This helps to make room for enough people, but still leave space for parks. Singapore is one of the busiest cities in the world and is home to six million people, yet 46 per cent of it is green space – the equivalent of over 80,000 football pitches!

Maths mistake: wobbly bridges

Most modern bridges are tested using a digital model to see what will happen in the real world – especially in wind, rain and even earthquakes. This helps engineers make sure their design is strong and stable.

Suspension bridges are especially difficult to design. These are bridges where the weight of the bridge is supported by cables connected to towers anchored to the ground. Because the bridge is suspended by cables, engineers expect there to be some up and down wobbling, so they design and test the bridge to make sure it's not damaged by this movement.

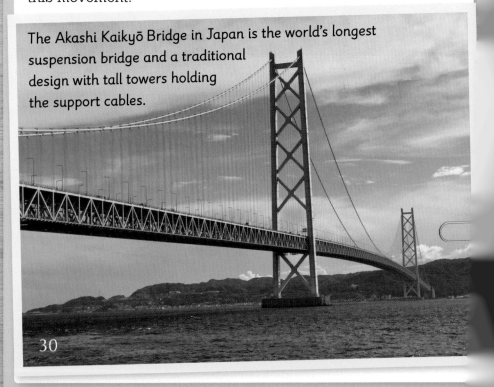

The Akashi Kaikyō Bridge in Japan is the world's longest suspension bridge and a traditional design with tall towers holding the support cables.

The Millennium Bridge, London

In 2000, the Millennium Bridge opened in London, UK. It had a unique design – its support cables were low down, to improve the view for pedestrians when they walked across it. But soon after opening, an unexpected problem appeared.

Like other bridges, how much it wobbled had been tested. However, because it didn't have high towers, when people walked across, their movements made the bridge wobble side to side, up to seven centimetres each way! No one thought this side-to-side wobbling was possible, and so the bridge hadn't been tested for it.

It took two years to repair the bridge. The Millennium Bridge no longer wobbles, but it's still called "The Wobbly Bridge" by many Londoners.

4 Saving lives

Did you know maths is used to keep people safe and healthy?

Can maths help you to stop catching a cold?

How diseases and illness spread can sometimes seem random. Some people will catch a cold, but other people won't. Some diseases spread faster in some places than others. However, if we collect lots of data, maths can be used to find patterns to help control diseases and save lives.

Doctors also use maths to check if new medicines and drugs work properly before they are given to the public. To do this, they give some people the real medicine and other people a pretend pill with nothing in it – this is called a placebo. They then compare what happens to these two groups of people. If only the people who took the medicine get better, then they know it was the medicine which helped them. These tests happen on very large groups of people, and it's how all new medicines are tested.

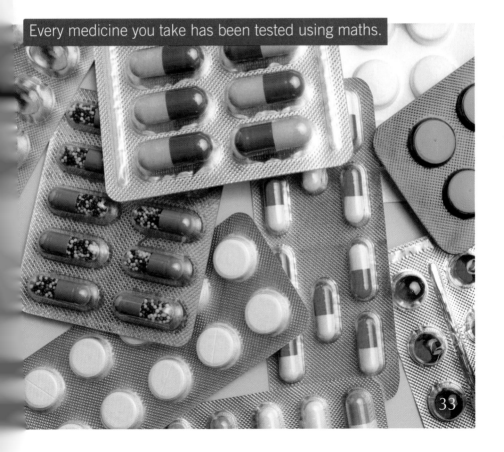

Every medicine you take has been tested using maths.

33

Mapping disease

In the 1800s, a new disease called cholera began spreading across London, and no one knew what was causing it. Some people thought it was caused by bad smells, and other people thought it was spread by piles of rubbish. A doctor called John Snow decided he would try to work out the real cause of this disease, so he did what no one had thought to do. He used maths and collected data!

Doctor Snow recorded all the people who got sick from cholera near where he worked and he marked where these sick people lived on a map. When he looked at this map, he saw a clear pattern. Right in the middle of where these ill people lived was a pump that provided drinking water!

Doctor Snow showed the government his data and asked for the pump to be closed. Sure enough, when it was closed, fewer people got sick. It was discovered that a nearby **cesspit** was leaking into the drinking water, causing cholera. Confusingly, some people far away from the pump also got sick. It turned out they liked the taste of the pump water and travelled miles to collect it!

Many lives were saved by Doctor Snow, all by looking at data on a map.

Doctor Snow's original map. Each black bar shows a patient sick with cholera. Most of these black bars can be found a short distance from the pump on Broad Street.

The maths nurse

In 1854, a young nurse called Florence Nightingale was sent to work in a British army hospital. She was shocked by what she found – the hospital was dirty, patients were not cleaned regularly and infections spread quickly between them.

Just like John Snow, Florence Nightingale decided to collect data to understand what was happening and how she could help.

For two years, she collected information about why soldiers died – if they died from battle wounds, or by infections they caught after arriving at the hospital. In the 1800s, most information about patients in hospitals was written down as long lists of numbers. These lists took a long time to read, and made it very difficult to see any patterns.

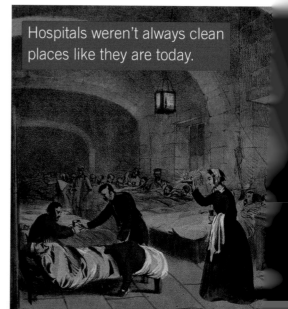

Hospitals weren't always clean places like they are today.

So Florence invented a new way to display this information – as graphs. These clearly showed that most soldiers weren't dying from battle wounds, but in the hospital from infections!

These graphs were impossible for the government to ignore, and so the hospital where she worked was soon cleaned up to stop infections spreading, saving thousands of lives. Florence Nightingale went on to improve hospitals all across the world, which wouldn't have been possible without maths!

The graph Florence designed. Each month has a bar, and its size shows how many people died that month.

Key
blue = preventable disease
black = other causes
red = wounds

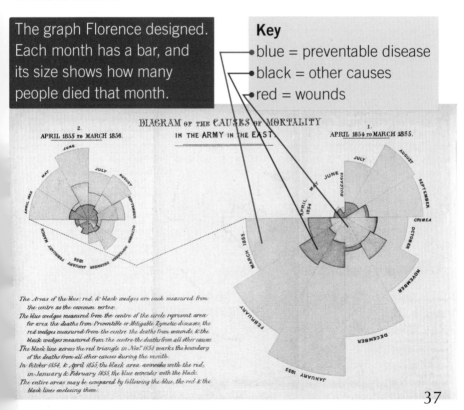

DIAGRAM of the CAUSES of MORTALITY
IN THE ARMY IN THE EAST.

2.
APRIL 1855 to MARCH 1856.

1.
APRIL 1854 to MARCH 1855.

The Areas of the blue, red, & black wedges are each measured from the centre as the common vertex.
The blue wedges measured from the centre of the circle represent area for area the deaths from Preventible or Mitigable Zymotic diseases, the red wedges measured from the centre the deaths from wounds, & the black wedges measured from the centre the deaths from all other causes.
The black line across the red triangle in Nov.ʳ 1854 marks the boundary of the deaths from all other causes during the month.
In October 1854, & April 1855, the black area coincides with the red, in January & February 1855, the blue coincides with the black.
The entire areas may be compared by following the blue, the red & the black lines enclosing them.

See how it spreads

Maths can also be used to predict how diseases might spread in the future. To do this, scientists make a simplified plan of how people connect to each other in the real world. This is called a mathematical model, and contains just the information important to studying diseases – things like the number of people that live in each place, how close they live to each other and what shared public spaces they use.

To see how a disease might spread between people in this simple model, scientists need to know a few things about a disease:

- How close do people need to be to each other to spread the disease?
- If someone catches it, how many more people will they spread it to?
- How quickly do people get better after catching it?
- How many people live in the area where the disease is spreading?

With this information, scientists can see how the disease spreads in this mathematical model, and use this information to help people to stop the disease in the real world.

Models can also be used to test what might help to fight a disease. Models were very important to work out how to manage the COVID-19 pandemic in the 2020s. This is how scientists discovered that wearing a mask was a good way to reduce the spread of infection, and also what distance was safe to stand near infected people.

There are lots of different ways to control diseases, but maths can be used to make sure the most lives are saved.

5 Maths in the driving seat

Computers make it much easier to use maths to improve the world. People like Florence Nightingale completed all their work by hand, but modern computers can do millions of calculations per second, easily beating even the best mathematical minds. In fact, the world's fastest computers can do a **trillion** calculations every second!

With such powerful computers, can we get rid of humans and leave maths in charge?

The Fugaku supercomputer in Kobe, Japan, can do 442,000,000,000,000,000 calculations every second!

A driverless future

When you walk or cycle outside, you use your senses to work out what is happening and where you can go. Your eyes look out for the path ahead, and if there are any obstacles in your way. Your ears listen out for noises which might be dangerous, like a car approaching behind you.

You use your senses to understand what is happening in the world.

Your brain then takes in all of this information, works out what to do next and moves your body. It does this hundreds of times every second without you really noticing!

Scientists have copied this idea to help build cars that can drive themselves. For that, maths is vital.

A self-driving car needs to sense its environment. Just like humans, they use a variety of different sensors. Video cameras on the front and back see traffic signs, traffic lights, cars and pedestrians on the road. Wheels can detect if they are too close to the curb. Most importantly, a self-driving car has a LiDAR sensor on the roof – this fires out a laser beam that bounces off objects and back to the car, telling it how far away things are.

a research car, with lots of sensors attached

All of these sensors send signals to the car's "brain", which is a central computer. This uses complicated maths to work out what is around the car, where the road is going, how fast other cars are driving and what is written on road signs. The driverless car uses this information to predict what it should do next – accelerate, brake or steer. By doing this thousands of times every second, it can drive itself!

Most car accidents are caused by human mistakes – people driving too fast, looking at their mobile phone, or driving when tired. Driverless cars could remove human mistakes from driving completely, and potentially save many lives in the future by putting maths in the driving seat!

Would you feel safe in a driverless car?

Drones to the rescue

The same maths and technology that's used to help cars to drive themselves is also being used to make **drones** fly themselves. These small flying machines could completely change the way we live our lives in the future.

Drones could deliver fresh food from a local restaurant to your door in minutes, and parcels directly from the shop.

Drones could also be used for more important things, such as responding quickly in first aid emergencies, delivering essential supplies to remote areas and even fighting forest fires. This would mean putting fewer people in dangerous situations.

a prototype delivery drone

45

Maths mistake: almost to Mars

In 1998, the Mars Climate Orbiter was launched, a spacecraft travelling towards Mars. It was planned not to land on Mars, but to travel around the planet and measure its weather.

Once a spacecraft is in space, scientists send sets of instructions to tell the craft how to move. This includes telling the spacecraft which engines to turn on, and for how long, in order to reach its destination safely. These instructions are basically a long list of mathematical code.

an illustration of the Mars Climate Orbiter above Mars

But even rocket scientists make mistakes! In this case, the team who'd built the Mars Climate Orbiter used imperial measurements – inches and feet – but one of the teams who sent instructions to the spacecraft used metric measurements – centimetres and metres.

This simple mistake meant that the spacecraft was sent too close to Mars. Instead of travelling around the planet, the Mars Climate Orbiter burnt up and crashed on it, destroying all the scientific instruments on board. Fortunately, this mistake hasn't been repeated again, and a number of spacecraft have been successfully sent to Mars, giving us a wealth of information about the planet, such as its climate.

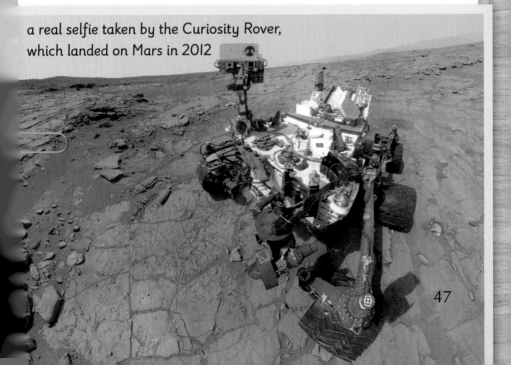

a real selfie taken by the Curiosity Rover, which landed on Mars in 2012

Virtual judges

You might not think it, but being a judge in a courtroom involves thinking mathematically. A judge takes in lots of different information, looks for patterns or similarities and then comes up with a final decision of what to do. But people in courtrooms still make mistakes! An important piece of evidence might be missed out, or worse, people might be lying.

To make courtrooms quicker and maybe fairer, researchers are developing virtual judges. These use mathematical models to scan through piles of paperwork, look for important facts and use this to suggest decisions.

Robot judges use something known as artificial intelligence, or AI. This is when a computer has something which seems like human intelligence – it can learn from experiences, respond to new information and make decisions by itself.

In Estonia, virtual judges are already being used to decide cases about crimes worth less than 7000 euros, like unpaid rent or damages caused in a car crash. People can still ask for a human judge to look over a decision if they are unhappy with the robot.

In the future, these AI models will work like a digital assistant on the judge's computer, reading paperwork and suggesting decisions, speeding up the work of a human judge.

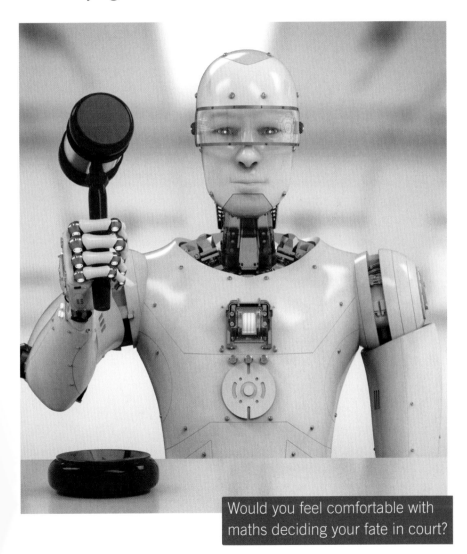

Would you feel comfortable with maths deciding your fate in court?

Cutting down crime

What if we could use maths to stop crimes before they happened, avoiding the need for a robot judge altogether?

Just like John Snow did with cholera, many police teams use a map to pinpoint where crimes happened. This means they can see where crimes often take place, and send more police officers to these areas. This might also show that car thefts are common in one part of town, but **vandalism** only happens in other parts.

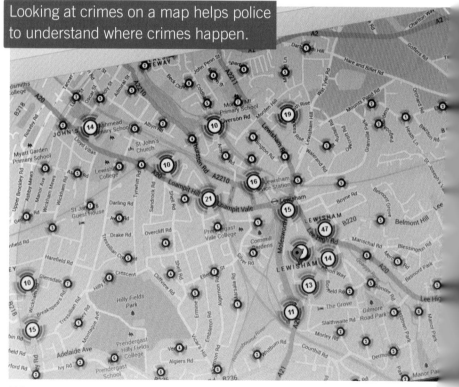

Looking at crimes on a map helps police to understand where crimes happen.

Police teams have lots of data about past crimes.
Some use maths to look for patterns and can then predict
what might happen next – all using AI.

AI computer programs can take in information about past
crimes, such as what happened, where it was and when it
happened, plus information about the location of things
in a city, such as banks, restaurants and major roads.
They are even given things like the weather forecast.
The AI programs use this information to predict where in
a city different types of crime might happen and when.

These AI programs can process information much quicker
and more accurately than people can. This means that
they should be able to predict where police officers will be
needed most, and keep places safer for everyone.

Using maths could help police officers
better support their communities.

51

6 Winning with maths

It's almost impossible to use maths to predict random events, but thankfully winning at sports mostly comes down to people's skill, and maths can definitely help with this. There are really two types of skill in sports and games. Your physical ability, like how fast you can run or cycle, and your understanding of the rules of the game, which is where maths comes in.

Many sportspeople, like cyclists, use maths to help them win.

On your bike!

Almost every aspect of professional cycling has been shaped by maths. Bicycle designs are tested in computer simulations to check they can move as quickly as possible. A rider's performance is measured, to see where they improve. Even the food a rider eats will be carefully examined to make sure they get exactly the right amount of energy before a race.

Mathematical football

Football is a very popular sport, and many teams now use maths to help beat their rivals. They do this by gathering huge amounts of data. Some of this is recorded by humans: people watching games and noting every time the ball was kicked, where it was and what happened to it. The top teams also use overhead cameras to record where players are, taking 25 photos every second. This gives teams a great amount of data to be studied.

In just one match, the ball is kicked over 2000 times!

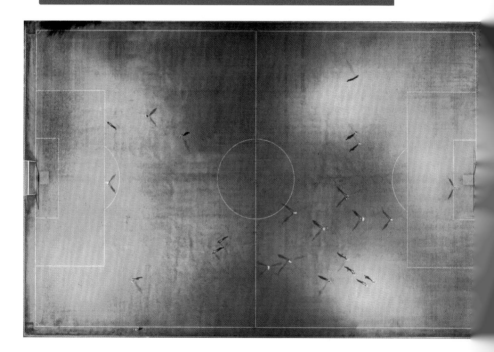

The main aim of playing football is to score goals, and maths can show you the best place to score one from. First you need data about every time someone tried to score a goal: where they kicked the ball from, and if they were successful or not. If you combine all this information and display it on a map of the pitch, it will show the ideal area to score a goal from. Players can then keep this in mind during a match to decide whether to take a shot at a goal or pass to another player who is in a better position.

After a match is over, managers will look at data to show their players what they should have done, so they can improve for the future.

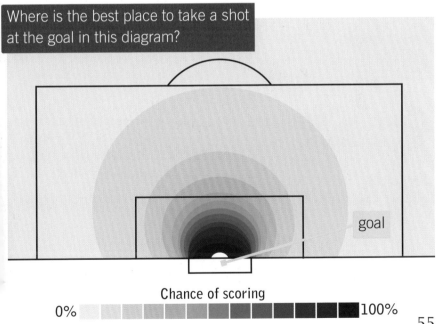

Where is the best place to take a shot at the goal in this diagram?

goal

Chance of scoring

0%   100%

Solving puzzles

If you've ever tried solving a Rubik's cube, you'll
know they are one of the most difficult puzzles
ever made. This is because there are 43 quintillion
(43,000,000,000,000,000,000) different ways a Rubik's
cube can be jumbled up! Amazingly, the world record to
solve one is just 3.47 seconds.

To solve a Rubik's cube, you need to follow an algorithm,
which is a list of instructions that need to be followed in
order to get a task done. Here's a simple algorithm to tell
a robot to brush its teeth:

1. Wet toothbrush

2. Put toothpaste on
   toothbrush

3. Brush top teeth for
   one minute

4. Brush bottom teeth
   for one minute

5. Spit out toothpaste

6. Rinse mouth with
   water

The algorithms for solving a Rubik's cube are more complicated than this, and people across the world have worked together to develop different ways of solving it. They usually involve starting with a set pattern like a cross of white tiles, and then working from this.

People have also coded robots to solve a Rubik's cube using these algorithms. They use cameras to see how the cube is jumbled, and mechanical arms to move the cube. The robots can think and move a cube much faster than humans, and so the record for a robot solving a Rubik's cube is an incredible 0.38 seconds!

Winning games

In 1770, people in Vienna were amazed when they saw something they thought was impossible – a robotic machine that could beat people at chess! This machine was actually controlled by a person hidden inside a box, but it got people thinking – could a machine ever beat people at a difficult game like chess?

Playing chess is even more complicated than solving a Rubik's cube – there are so many different ways a game could end that mathematicians can't even work out how many ways are possible! In fact, almost every game of chess that's played has never been seen before.

The "automaton chess player", was actually a robotic puppet, controlled by someone squeezed inside this table.

In 1997, a machine did finally beat a chess world champion. It was a computer called Deep Blue and it was two metres tall.

At each move in chess, a player needs to think about all the possible moves they could make, and how their opponent would respond to these. To help them plan their moves, champion chess players think back to all the different games they have played and what moves worked well.

Deep Blue was programmed with algorithms based on previous games won by champion chess players. It could consider 200 million possible moves every second, giving it the advantage it needed to win.

World champion Garry Kasparov plays chess against a computer, Deep Blue.

Maths mistake: running the distance

Marathons are one of the hardest sporting events that the general public can enter, with runners covering 42.2 kilometres over the course of a few hours. Organisers of the 2021 Brighton Marathon in the UK made their race even harder, however, by accidentally adding an extra 568 metres to the route!

Although the route had been carefully measured out, the mistake happened simply because someone put a marker cone a little too far up a hill on one part of the course.

The same organisers have even made the opposite mistake: in 2015, Brighton Marathon realised their half marathon course was actually 146 metres too short!

Runners race along the seafront at Brighton.

Measurement mistakes have even happened in the Olympic Games. In the 2000 Sydney Games, gymnastics officials accidentally set up the vaulting table five centimetres too low. This small difference caused chaos for competitors, with gold medal favourite Russian, Svetlana Khorkina, falling and injuring herself. The mistake was only spotted by one of the competitors in the middle of the competition, and everyone was offered the chance of vaulting again, but it was too late for Svetlana Khorkina who missed out on the chance of a medal due to her injury.

Gymnast Svetlana Khorkina performing at the 2000 Sydney Olympic Games.

7 Mathematical fun

You take your seat and the lights go down. It is silent. Suddenly, from nowhere, a huge explosion erupts in front of you, with flames bursting out towards you and a deafening noise ringing in your ears. In the distance, you can hear the fluttering sound of a superhero's cape as they fly over your head to help.

But there's no need to worry, because you are safely sitting in a cinema enjoying a movie – one of the many ways maths is used to have fun!

Mathematics is used to create realistic animated characters, and place them alongside actual humans in films.

Movie mayhem

All of the special effects in modern movies are made by maths. These are called CGI (computer generated imagery), because very powerful computers are used to run the complicated mathematical models that make the effects seem so realistic.

Believable CGI is created with a combination of maths and art. Maths is used to model what would happen in the real world, like a building collapsing, and art is used to imagine the impossible, like that collapse being caused by a giant alien.

Maths helps make the impossible seem possible.

If filmmakers want to make a scene of a giant alien knocking down a building, special effects teams start by studying what happens in the real world. How do buildings collapse? What happens to bricks when they crash? How do animals that are similar to the alien move? All this data is collected and combined to make a computer model of this impossible scene happening.

This model will then be tweaked to make the action as exciting as possible. Real-life events are rarely as loud or exciting as they appear in the movies – special effects artists add extra sounds and explosions to them to make them even more of a spectacle for cinemagoers to enjoy!

Exploring new worlds

Virtual reality (VR) also uses CGI, but takes it a step further. VR computer games allow players to interact with the virtual world through VR headsets, looking all around a CGI world and not just at a cinema screen in front of them.

But VR isn't just used for fun – some hospitals use it to train surgeons on difficult operations before they work on real people.

VR can immerse you in new worlds.

But what if you could change the real world, and not just a VR world? Augmented reality (AR) can do this. AR headsets use cameras and sensors similar to those in a self-driving car, to scan and build a model of the world around you. When you look through an AR headset, you see a view of the real world as if you're looking through glasses, but with CGI elements placed on top, such as dinosaurs running past your house!

AR can also be used for more practical things like showing you the weather forecast when you look up at the sky, seeing what a new pair of trainers looks like on your feet and even helping you find your way around a new city.

Augmented reality is already used in many mobile phone apps.

Maths music

You probably enjoy listening to music, but did you know that music is basically just data? It might sound natural and artistic, but when music is written down it's a set of simple instructions – an algorithm. It tells musicians which note to play, when to play it and how loudly.

In 1897, the first piano was made that could play itself. This was before computers were invented, and the piano was controlled by sheets of card with holes telling the piano which notes to play. These were called "punch cards" and were a very early type of algorithm – they stored a set of instructions that a machine followed in order to make something happen.

This piano plays itself by reading the punch card you can see.

Today, mathematicians are making AI programs which can write brand new music – in the style of any band or singer!

To write a new song that sounds like your favourite band or singer, all you need to do is give the AI lots of examples of songs by them. It will search through these for patterns, making a set of "rules" that all these songs follow.
The AI can use these rules to make a completely new song that still sounds like your chosen band. No one tells the AI what the rules are – it will work it out by looking for patterns.

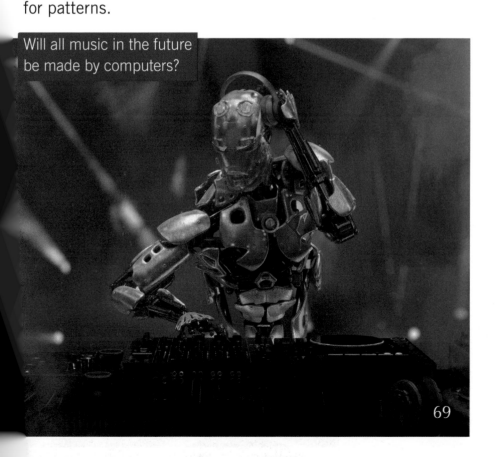

Will all music in the future be made by computers?

8 Who is in control?

If an ancient Egyptian from 3000 BCE could visit our world today, they would be astonished by how much our mathematical skills have grown from their simple understanding of shape and volume needed to build the Pyramids. We can now use maths to give our cities the best designs, save lives and even build virtual worlds.

More and more data about how we live our lives is being collected, in the hope that this can improve the world for the better. Every part of our lives is helped by thinking mathematically.

We're moving into a future where much of our personal lives is data – information about your health, where you live and where you have been, even the foods you enjoy or movies you like!

This data is kept by large companies, and it's important to remember to keep it safe by only using companies that can be trusted and having strong passwords to avoid it being stolen.

In just over 2000 years, humans have gone from using maths to build pyramids to creating complex data centres to store our information.

But what about the AI models that run things without humans being involved? How do we make sure they only do what they are programmed to? In 2019, a hotel in Japan replaced its AI-powered robot staff with people again. Why? The AI assistants were waking guests at night because they thought the sound of snoring was people asking questions!

And if we let computers take over too much of our society, will we slowly lose skills, such as being able to drive cars ourselves? Maths may make incredible things like driverless cars and chess-playing computers possible, but that doesn't mean we should accept all these changes into our lives without carefully thinking how things will change as a result. Maths can improve the lives of everyone, but we may not want it to take over completely.

Almost every part of your life is creating new data.

Over to you!

Thinking mathematically is a skill that anyone can use. You just need to take some time to look deeper at the world around you. Next time you're outside, you could try to use maths to explore your world. Are the trees taller on one side of your road than the other? How many people walk past your home every hour? What does this tell you about where you live?

All around the world, mathematicians are asking questions like this too, expanding our understanding of everything around us, and changing things for the better.

If you want to help create a safer, fairer and more enjoyable world for everyone, have you thought about becoming a mathematician? You might be surprised to see where maths can take you!

How might you use maths to improve the world?

Glossary

accountants people who keep track of money for a company

bronze a strong and heavy metal, made by melting together the metals copper and tin

cesspit a large hole where people emptied their toilet waste, before flushing toilets were invented

city-state a small country that's made up of just one city

civilisation a complex and organised community of people, with government, writing and technology

drones small flying vehicles without a pilot

engineers people who use maths and science to design and build things

evaporates when a liquid is heated up, boils and becomes a gas

global warming when carbon dioxide and other polluting gases trap heat from the Sun in our atmosphere and cause the planet to warm up

hurricanes powerful rotating storms that form over the ocean and move over land, damaging buildings

mathematicians people who use maths to solve problems

pedestrians people who move around by walking or running

philosophers people who attempt to understand big questions about humans and the universe and discuss this with others

satellites machines which are launched into space with a rocket, then orbit around Earth

structures things designed and built to be used by humans – including buildings, bridges, railways, roads and dams

theories ideas to explain how things in the world work

tornadoes strong twisting columns of air which form on land during a thunderstorm

trillion a million million, or 1,000,000,000,000

urban an area of land that's been built on, filled with houses, shops, roads and other structures, such as towns and cities

vandalism destroying or damaging someone else's property

Index

A city built by maths

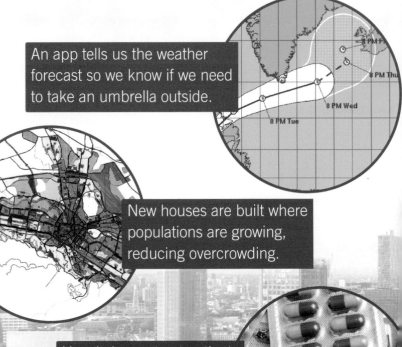

An app tells us the weather forecast so we know if we need to take an umbrella outside.

New houses are built where populations are growing, reducing overcrowding.

Hospitals can treat patients with the latest safe and effective treatments.

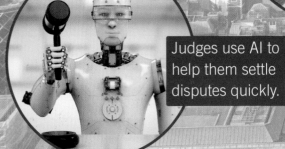

Judges use AI to help them settle disputes quickly.

Train stations safely schedule hundreds of trains every day.

Streets can be made car-free, without creating traffic on other streets.

Police officers are sent to areas where they are needed most.

Football teams improve their chances of winning.

Cinemas take us to realistic new worlds.

Bridges can be built without wobbles!

Ideas for reading

Written by Gill Matthews
Primary Literacy Consultant

Reading objectives:
- check that the book makes sense to them, discussing their understanding and exploring the meaning of words in context
- ask questions to improve their understanding
- summarise the main ideas drawn from more than one paragraph, identifying key details that support the main ideas
- identify how language, structure and presentation contribute to meaning
- retrieve, record and present information from non-fiction

Spoken language objectives:
- ask relevant questions to extend their understanding and knowledge
- use spoken language to develop understanding through speculating, hypothesising, imagining and exploring ideas
- participate in discussions, presentations, performances, role play, improvisations and debates

Curriculum links: Maths – Statistics

Interest words: simple, complex, incredible, deeper

Build a context for reading

- Ask children to explore the covers of the book. Discuss what they expect to learn from the book.
- Focus on the final sentence in the back-cover blurb. Ask children how many different ways they think maths is used in the world.
- Ask what kind of organisational features the children expect to find in the book. Give them time to skim through the book to find the contents, glossary and index. Ask children what the purpose of these features is and how they are organised.

Understand and apply reading strategies

- Read pp2–9 aloud, asking children to follow and to think about how the information is being presented. Take feedback and discuss the different visuals that have been used, for example, photos, painting, graphs, charts. Establish that it is sometimes easier to present information in a visual format rather than a written format.